FIRST FESTIVALS

Christmas

FIRST FESTIVALS

Christmas

Lois Rock

LION
Children's Books

Introduction

Text and artefacts by Lois Rock
Illustrations copyright © 1999 Helen Cann
Music arrangements copyright © 1998 Philip Tebbs
Photography by John Williams Studios, Thame
This edition copyright © 2003 Lion Hudson

The moral rights of the author and illustrator
have been asserted

A Lion Children's Book
an imprint of
Lion Hudson plc
Mayfield House, 256 Banbury Road,
Oxford OX2 7DH, England
www.lionhudson.com
ISBN 0 7459 4652 6

First hardback edition 1999
First paperback edition 2003
10 9 8 7 6 5 4 3 2 1

A catalogue record for this book is available
from the British Library

Typeset in 18/21 Baskerville MT Schlbk
Printed and bound in Singapore

Acknowledgments
Bible passage on page 1 from Isaiah 9:2, 6–7. Scriptures
quoted from the Good News Bible published by The Bible
Societies/HarperCollins Publishers Ltd, UK © American Bible
Society 1966, 1971, 1976, 1992, used with permission.

This book is one of a series dealing with the Christian festivals.

This one is about the best-loved of them all: the celebration of Christmas.

Here are traditional crafts to mark the season, from the looking-forward time of Advent to Christmas Day itself, with its gifts, greetings cards and decorations.

Here, too, is the story of the Nativity that lies at the heart of the festival, carols that sing out the story of Jesus' birth and tales from the Christian tradition that have shaped the customs of the season.

Contents

Advent

November nights are long and dark; in December, the nights are even longer.

As wintertime grows cold and bleak, those people who celebrate Christmas begin to look forward to a festive time at the end of the year: a celebration that is full of light and warmth and cheerfulness.

Christians call this season of waiting 'Advent'—a word which means 'coming'.

Advent begins four Sundays before Christmas.

As the weeks of Advent go by, Christians remember stories of long ago—stories of the Jewish people. Then, the Jews were a people who had been beaten in many wars. They were no longer free in the land they called their home. They believed that God had promised to send a special king who would lead them to freedom.

The coming of that king would be like a celebration after a long, dark winter.

A promise of a king

The people who walked in darkness have seen a great light.
They lived in a land of shadows, but now light is shining on them.
A child is born to us!
A son is given to us!
And he will be our ruler.
He will be called 'Wonderful Counsellor', 'Mighty God', 'Eternal Father',
   'Prince of Peace'.
His royal power will continue to grow; his kingdom will always be at peace.

From the book of the prophet Isaiah, in the Bible

2 Advent Ring

Here is a traditional Christian decoration for Advent. It helps count the four Sundays in Advent that lead up to Christmas.

On the first Sunday, people light one candle in the ring. As it burns, they may read or remember some of the words from the Bible in which God promises to send a king who will set people free.

On the second Sunday, they light two candles; on the third, they light three, and on the fourth they light four.

On Christmas Day, they light the centre candle as they remember the birth of the one they believe was God's king— the one they call 'Christ', the baby Jesus.

You will need

large garden saucer

damp soil or sand

5 small flowerpots

4 red candles

1 tall white candle

sprigs of evergreens such as fir, holly and ivy

1 Fill the garden saucer with soil or sand. Wedge four flowerpots in a circle around the edge, and another in the centre. Half fill these with soil or sand.

2 Put the red candles in the pots round the edge, and the white candle in the centre pot.

3 Push evergreen sprigs into the sand to cover it. Take care to keep the leaves below the rim of the pots, so they will not catch fire as the candles burn.

3 Advent Calendar

An Advent calendar helps count the days to Christmas. This one, like many, counts from 1 December to Christmas Day on 25 December.

There is a hidden surprise for every day in Advent.

1 Draw a simple Christmas tree shape. The one here was 70 cm tall including the pot. Ask a grown-up to help you cut it out, using a craft knife against a ruler on a cutting mat.

2 Mark equally spaced lines to show where the yarn will go. Cut notches where these lines meet the edge of the tree.

3 Paint the tree green and the pot red. Leave to dry.

4 Wind fuzzy yarn around the tree, using the notches as guides. Hold the beginning and end of the yarn in place with sticky tape on the wrong side of the card.

You will need

large sheet of thick card

pencil and ruler

cutting mat and craft knife

green and red acrylic paint

paintbrushes

fuzzy yarn

sticky tape

scissors

This Advent calendar is shaped like a Christmas tree. The plain envelopes each contain a paper decoration. Unwrap one decoration each day and hang it on the tree.

Make an extra special star to put on the top for Christmas Day. Use tape or sticky putty to hold it in place.

4 Decorations

Here's how to make bright decorations and envelopes for your Advent calendar tree.

Decorations

You will need

thin card

pencil

scissors

strong paper in lots of bright colours

coloured yarn

sticky tape

1 Draw shapes like the ones shown here onto thin card and cut them out. Use the templates at the back of this book as guides.

2 One at a time, hold a shape against a piece of strong paper and tear it little by little along the edges to get the same shape. Tear out all the shapes you need to make 25 decorations!

3 Glue the shapes together to make decorations.

4 Cut yarn in 15 cm lengths and fold each in half. Tape a piece to each decoration on the wrong side, with the cut ends free so you can tie the decoration onto your tree.

Envelopes

You will need

large sheets of red paper

gold coloured paper-clips

ruler and pencil

scissors

gold pen

gold stickers

1 Use a ruler and pencil to mark squares on the red paper. The squares for the envelopes shown here were 9 cm x 9 cm.

2 Place a ruler along each line and tear the paper firmly along it. Tear the marked paper first into strips, and then the strips into mini squares.

3 Fold each square in half and in half again. Hold the folded paper with the central point towards you, and snip a tiny piece off the two side corners but not the top one.

4 Unfold it. There will be a notch in the middle of each side. Lay your decoration in the centre of the square, then fold in each point over it, folding from notch to notch.

5 Sticker the envelope shut to hold the points together.

6 Number each envelope from 1 to 25. You are now ready to hang them on the tree in order, from the bottom of the tree to the top, using a paper-clip on the yarn (see the picture on page 3).

The story at the heart of Christmas is the story of the birth of Jesus. The people who believe he was God's special king—the Christ—call themselves Christians. Christmas ('Christ-mas') is the name of their festival.

Mary and the angel

Long ago, in the town of Nazareth in Palestine, lived a young woman named Mary. Like all the girls her age, she was planning to get married. The man who was going to be her husband was called Joseph.

One day, an angel appeared to Mary. 'Greetings,' said the angel. 'I bring special news. God has chosen you to bear a child—the king for whom your people are waiting. You are to call him Jesus.'

Mary was puzzled and dismayed. 'How can I be a mother?' she asked. 'I'm not yet a wife!'

'God can make this come true,' said the angel; and Mary agreed to do as God wanted.

The birth of Jesus

Months went by. The time was coming when Mary's baby would be born. Then came an announcement from the emperor who ruled the land. He wanted to know exactly how many people lived in his empire, so he could ask them to pay taxes. Everyone was ordered to go to their home town to put their names on a list.

So Joseph took Mary from Nazareth to Bethlehem. Many people were travelling for the same reason. In crowded Bethlehem, the only place where Mary and Joseph could find shelter was a stable.

There, Mary's baby was born. Mary wrapped the child in swaddling bands and laid him to sleep in a manger.

Away in a Manger

A - way in a — man - ger, no — crib for a bed, The — lit - tle Lord Je - sus laid — down his sweet head. The stars in the — bright sky looked — down where he lay, The — lit - tle Lord Je - sus a - sleep on the hay.

The cattle are lowing, the baby awakes,
But little Lord Jesus, no crying he makes.
I love thee, Lord Jesus! Look down from the sky,
And stay by my side until morning is nigh.

Be near me, Lord Jesus, I ask thee to stay
Close by me for ever, and love me, I pray.
Bless all the dear children in thy tender care,
And fit us for heaven to live with thee there.

The shepherds on the hillside

On the same night that Mary's baby was born, there were some shepherds out on the hillside near Bethlehem. They were watching over their sheep.

Suddenly, an angel appeared. The shepherds were terrified.

'Do not be afraid,' said the angel. 'I bring you good news, and the good news is for everyone. You know that Bethlehem is the town where your great King David was born, long ago. Tonight, God's special king has been born there: the Christ has come.

'Go and find out for yourselves that what I am saying is true. You will find the baby wrapped in swaddling bands and lying in a manger.'

Then a great crowd of angels appeared. They sang songs of praise:

'Glory to God in the highest, and peace on earth.'

When the angels had gone, the shepherds looked at one another in amazement. 'Let us go to Bethlehem, and see what has happened,' they said.

So they went, and they found Mary and the baby, just as the angel had said.

While Shepherds Watched Their Flocks

While shep - herds watched their flocks by night, All
seat - ed on the ground, The an - gel of the
Lord came down, And glo - ry shone a - round.

'Fear not,' said he, for mighty dread
Had seized their troubled mind;
'Glad tidings of great joy I bring
To you and all mankind.

'To you in David's town this day
Is born of David's line
A saviour who is Christ the Lord;
And this shall be the sign:

'The heavenly babe you there shall find
To human view displayed,
All meanly wrapped in swathing bands,
And in a manger laid.'

Thus spake the seraph and forthwith
Appeared a shining throng
Of angels praising God, who thus
Addressed their joyful song:

'All glory be to God on high,
And on the earth be peace;
Goodwill henceforth from heaven to men
Begin and never cease.'

7 The Christmas Story

The wise men

When Jesus was born in Bethlehem, a man named Herod was king. His palace was in the nearby city of Jerusalem.

Some men who studied the stars came to Jerusalem from lands to the east of the city. They had an important question for the people there: 'Where is the baby who is born to be your king? We have seen his star and have come to worship him.'

King Herod heard of their search, and he was at once angry. He hated anyone who threatened his power. So he called together his chief priests and teachers. 'You have studied the ancient writings of our people,' he said. 'They tell us that one day God will send us a special king—the Christ. Where will the Christ be born?'

'In Bethlehem,' they replied.

Then Herod called the travellers from the east to a secret meeting, and asked them what they knew about the star and when they had first seen it. When he had found out all they knew, he sent them to Bethlehem.

'Search for the king there,' he told them, 'and then come and tell me where he is.'

So the men left. They saw the star ahead of them. It stopped right over the place where the baby was. They went in and found the baby with his mother Mary.

Then they gave the gifts they had brought: gold and frankincense and myrrh.

Afterwards, they went back to their own land. In a dream, God told them not to go back to Herod, so they chose a different way home.

We Three Kings

We three kings of O-ri-ent are; Bear-ing gifts we tra-vel a-far. Field and foun-tain, moor and moun-tain, fol-low-ing yon-der star. O___ star of won-der, star of night, Star with roy-al beau-ty bright, West-ward lead-ing, still pro-ceed-ing, Guide us to thy per-fect light.

Melchior:

Born a king on Bethlehem plain,
Gold I bring to crown him again,
King for ever, ceasing never
Over us all to reign. (*Chorus*)

Caspar:

Frankincense to offer have I,
Incense owns a deity nigh;
Prayer and praising, all men raising,
Worship him, God most high! (*Chorus*)

Balthazar:

Myrrh is mine, its bitter perfume
Breathes a life of gathering gloom;
Sorrowing, sighing, bleeding, dying,
Sealed in the stone-cold tomb. (*Chorus*)

Glorious now behold him arise,
King and God and sacrifice,
Alleluia, alleluia,
Earth to the heavens replies. (*Chorus*)

8 A Nativity Scene

The Christmas story of the birth of Jesus is often called the Nativity. The word means 'birth'. Some people act out the story in Nativity plays at Christmas. Some set up a model of what happened in the story—a Nativity scene.

A stable

You will need

cardboard box

craft knife or strong scissors

marvin medium

white and brown acrylic paints

paintbrushes

straight twigs

strip of clear acetate film (overhead projector film is good)

gold card

sticky tape

pencil

1 Mix some marvin medium into each of the acrylic paint colours you are using. Brush over the stable. You will need to let each coat dry before adding more paint. Apply as many coats as you need to hide any writing on the box. Paint the outside dark and the inside a bit lighter.

2 Put a thick layer of marvin medium on the 'roof' and lay straight twigs well into it. Leave to dry.

3 Draw a star on gold card and cut it out. Cut a strip of acetate and tape the star onto one end. Then tape the other end to the inside front of the stable.

9 Nativity Characters

You will need

thick card

thin white card

pencil

pencil crayons

scissors

plain and patterned paper
in different colours

glue

paper clips

double-sided tape

1 Copy the shapes at the back of this book onto thick card and cut them out. They are a figure, a tunic and a skirt shape.

2 Fold the thin white card in half and lay the figure shape on it, with the top of the head on the fold. Draw round this shape on white card to make as many figures as you need. Cut them out.

6 Draw round the shape for the tunic on a folded piece of coloured paper (to give a front and a back) and the shape for the skirt on a single piece of paper. Then cut them out. Make clothes for all the figures in this way.

7 Wrap a skirt around the leg part of each figure and tape it in place. Spread glue on the wrong side of the tunic pieces, from the neck down to the bottom of the sleeves. Glue the front and back tunic pieces onto each figure.

3 Colour in the hands, feet and head. Colour the back and the front.

4 Open up the figure shape and put double-sided tape along the arms and the head on the inside. Fold the figure right side out and press the tape to stick the top part of the figure together.

5 Fold the tabs at the bottom of each figure inwards and overlap them. Glue them together to make a base that will allow the figure to stay upright.

8 Add extra details if you wish. The belt is made by stitching a piece of yarn through the figure at waist level and tying a knot. The angel's wings are cut from a doily and taped on the back.

9 Make a manger from brown paper. Cut a rectangle 8 cm x 5 cm and fold in 15 mm along each side. Make snips as shown along the long creases to where they cross the short creases.

10 Fold up the sides and glue in place. Fill it with straw made from snipped paper and add a baby that you draw on thin card and cut out.

10 Christmas Gifts

Many stories are told of what Jesus did when he was grown-up. He spent his days telling people about God. He said that the God who made the world is kind, loving and forgiving. He said that the right way for people to live is to love God, and to be kind and forgiving to everyone around them. Many people listened to what Jesus had to say. Ever since, many, many people have tried to live as he taught. Here is a story of one of them.

The story of Saint Nicholas

Long ago, in the town of Myra, lived a man named Nicholas, He was the leader of the Christian community, and everyone knew him as a good and generous man.

In the town lived a poor family where there were three daughters. They were all old enough to get married. However, it was the tradition that a bride must bring a gift of money to her new family… and their father had none. No one wanted to marry them, and they were very sad.

Nicholas heard of their sorrow. He gathered together some gold coins. One dark night, he crept round to where the sisters lived, and threw the coins in through an open window.

The coins landed by the hearth, where the sisters had left their wet clothes to dry. In the morning, they found gold coins among their shoes and stockings—gifts that would enable them to get married and live happily.

Nicholas did many good deeds like this. He was so good, that people called him a saint: Saint Nicholas, or Santa Claus!

To this day many people hang up stockings on Christmas Eve, and on Christmas morning find that they have been filled with good things by a gift-giver who comes in secret.

Stockings

Here are Christmas stockings to decorate.

Will you hang a stocking at the foot of your bed on Christmas Eve, and will you find it full of gifts in the morning?

Will you be a gift-giver, and help fill a stocking secretly for someone you love?

You will need

long knitted socks in bright colours

bright yarns, buttons and beads

tapestry needle

1 Thread your needle with your first choice of bright yarn. Pull the two ends even. Push the needle through the folded cuff at a place where you want to put a tuft.

2 Take care to keep your other hand in the opening, so you don't stitch the opening up! Pull the needle through, leaving a tail of yarn about 10 cm long on the right side. Then push the needle back about 5 mm away.

3 Cut the thread to leave another tail about 10 cm long.

4 Tie the ends with a reef knot: wind the right thread over the left and pull snugly, then left over right and pull tight.

5 Snip the tails to leave a tuft about 2 cm long. Make tufts over the cuff in your choice of colours.

6 You can use the same method to tie on beads or buttons. Work from the inside to the outside and, using a single piece of yarn, thread a bead or button before taking the needle back to the inside. Tie off the ends on the inside and snip them to about 2 cm long.

12 The Christmas Tree

Decorating a tree with lights and pretty things is one of the best-loved Christmas traditions. Here is one story about why the tradition began.

The child and the fir tree

Long ago, a man named Boniface set off through Europe on a special journey. In the lands where he was travelling, people had never heard the story of Jesus. They did not believe in a God of love and gentleness. Some of the customs they followed were harsh and cruel.

One night, Boniface came across a gathering in the forest. People stood around a mighty oak tree. Tied to its trunk was a frightened child.

'What is going on?' Boniface wanted to know.

'The child must be killed, and offered as a sacrifice to our gods,' came the answer.

Boniface was dismayed. 'Please wait,' he asked. 'I believe that the great God of heaven and earth does not want this child to be killed. I want to tell you of a man named Jesus, who travelled this world hundreds of years ago showing people all the love and goodness of God.'

What he said made the people change their minds. When they had finished listening, they allowed Boniface to untie the child. They agreed to have the oak tree cut down.

By its roots was a little fir tree. 'The oak that you used for your old customs is gone,' he said. 'This tree is a symbol of your new belief, as followers of Jesus.'

13 Gingerbread Hearts

These simple tree decorations are spicy cookies. Their heart shape and their sweetness are a reminder of the love people can show each other.

Christmas is a time to remember that Jesus told his followers to love one another.

You will need

75 g brown sugar

30 ml golden syrup

15 ml black treacle

15 ml water

100 g margarine

1 tsp cinnamon

1 tsp ginger

250 g self-raising flour

extra flour

2 bowls

mixing spoon

rolling pin

drinking straws

baking parchment

heart-shaped cookie cutters

baking trays

wire rack

yarn

> ☺ *Ask a grown-up to help you cook. Have them preheat the oven to 160 °C.*
>
> ☺ *Always wash your hands before you begin.*

| Put the sugar, syrup, treacle, water and margarine into a bowl. Microwave on high for 2 minutes. Stir and microwave for 1 minute more.

5 Put a large sheet of baking parchment on a clean worksurface and sprinkle some extra flour on it. Roll the dough to 4 mm thick with a rolling pin.

6 Line a baking tray with baking parchment. Use a heart-shaped cutter to cut out your cookies. Lay them on the lined baking tray.

2 Put the flour and spices in another bowl and mix.

3 Stir the microwaved ingredients till they are liquid, then add this to the bowl of dry ingredients.

4 Stir till the mixture forms lumps, then use your hands to mix it so it forms a ball of dough.

7 Use a straw like a mini cutter to cut a hole in each cookie through which to thread your hanging loop. Press the end into the cookie and twist it slightly to lift out the tiny circle of dough (which will be pushed up into the straw).

8 Bake the cookies for 10 minutes or until they are just going dark at the edges. Ask a grown-up to lift them out of the oven and leave them on the tray till they are firm. Then lift them onto a wire rack to finish cooling.

9 Cut 30 cm lengths of yarn and fold them in half. Thread the looped end through the hanging hole of each heart, and then thread the dangling end through this loop. You can now use the ends to tie the cookie onto the tree.

14 Woven Hearts

These woven paper hearts are a traditional decoration. The colours chosen here stand for heaven and earth—a reminder of the Christian belief that Jesus was God's Son, come from heaven to show God's love on earth.

You will need

thick card

pencil and ruler

coloured paper

scissors

needle and yarn

1 Copy the shape shown at the back of this book onto thick card and cut it out. Mark the centre line as shown. Snip each side of the pencil line and pull away the thin curl of card in the middle.

2 Fold the coloured paper in half, wrong side showing. Lay the thick card with the flat end exactly on the crease and draw round it. Mark the centre line as well.

5 Next hold the folded end of the right-hand strip as you pull it through. Open up the fold and loop the strip over the upper strip of the left-hand shape.

6 Push the right-hand piece down so it settles into the slit on the left for the second part of the weaving. Take the top strip of the right-hand shape, open up the folded edge and loop it over the strip on the left.

3 Cut out the coloured shape and snip ONCE along the centre line. Make shapes in different colours. Refold each one with the right side out.

4 Now begin weaving. Take two shapes of different colours and hold one in each hand with the folded ends facing. Push the lower strip of the shape in your right hand in between the two layers of the strip in your left.

7 Next, fold the edge of the right-hand strip closed again and push it through the left-hand shape. Jiggle the paper so the weaving fits snugly.

8 Thread a hanging loop through all thicknesses.

Many people send cards at Christmas—to tell their family and friends that they love and remember them, and perhaps to tell them some news.

You will need

strong tracing paper or clear acetate film

stick of repositionable glue

craft knife and cutting mat

pencil and ruler

coloured card

acrylic paint

stencil brushes

block of polystyrene

thick needle

needle and thread

double-sided sticky tape

beads

scrap paper

1 On the coloured card, measure a rectangle as tall as the size of card you want and three times as wide. Cut it out, using a craft knife against a ruler on a cutting mat.

2 Mark the card into three panels along the top and bottom edges. Lay the ruler on the card to join them, and score lightly down this line with the craft knife. Fold the card up along this line, keeping the ruler in place to make the crease straight.

3 Draw a stencil design for your card on the tracing paper or acetate film. Cut out the stencil design using the craft knife on the cutting mat.

4 Spread a little glue on the back of the stencil, then lay the stencil on the middle panel of the card where you want the design to go. Put some paint on a saucer and dab the stencil brush into it. Dab the paint on the stencil hole, taking care not to damage the edges of the stencil.

5 Peel the stencil away and let the card dry. Blot the back of the stencil on scrap paper before using it to make other cards in the same way.

6 Decide where you want to put beads on the card— like the glittery beads that add sparkle to the star, or the decorations on the tree. Open up the card and lay it on the polystyrene block. Use the thick needle to make holes where the beads will go.

7 Thread a thinner needle and tape the end of the thread on the inside of the card near a hole. Then bring the needle to the front through a hole, pick up a bead, and take the needle back through the hole. Take the needle to the next hole and do the same till the holes all have beads. Tape the end of the thread firmly on the inside.

8 Fold the front panel of the card inwards so that it covers the back of the middle panel. Tape it in place with double-sided tape.

16 Christmas News

At Christmas, it's good to have news about family and friends. Christians also like to hear again the news about Jesus and to share it with others.

Here is a Christmas carol which does just that.

Go, Tell It on the Mountain

Go tell it on the moun - tain, Ov - er the hills and
ev - 'ry - where, ___ Go tell it on the moun - tain That
Je - sus Christ is born. While shep-herds kept their
watch - ing Ov - er wander - ing flocks by night, Be -
hold from out of hea - ven, There shone a ho - ly light. ___

(Chorus)
And lo, when they had seen it,
They all bowed down and prayed,
They travelled on together
To where the babe was laid.
(Chorus)

17 Gift Wrapping

You can hide any shape of gift in this clever bag.

You will need

scissors

wrapping paper

sticky tape

hole punch

gift ribbon

gift, loosely wrapped in tissue paper

1 Cut a rectangle of wrapping paper large enough to go loosely round the gift, with plenty of extra top and bottom.

2 Lay the paper wrong-side up and fold the sides so they overlap in the middle. Tape the join and crease the side edges firmly.

6 Unfold the top and put the gift inside. Then refold the top and tape shut.

7 Taking care not to damage the gift inside, punch a hole in each corner of the bag.

3 Fold a small triangle in at each of the bottom corners, and fold the lower edge up. Tape in place.

4 Now open up the top of the bag and bring the side creases together. Crease the new sides for a few centimetres down from the top.

5 Fold triangles in on these new sides and then fold down the top edge. Crease firmly but do not tape.

8 Thread gift ribbon through each hole and tie a knot. Tie it into bows or curl it.

Just think of all the ways you can wrap gifts to make them look really festive.

It's a good idea to add a tag to each gift, saying who it is for and who it is from.

You will need

bright card

scissors

hole punch

gift ribbon

pen

1 Cut a simple shape from bright card.

2 Punch a hole in the tag.

3 Add your message.

4 Tie the tag in with the wrap.

We Wish You a Merry Christmas

We wish you a mer-ry Christ-mas, We wish you a mer-ry Christ-mas, We wish you a mer-ry Christ-mas And a hap-py New Year.

Good ti-dings we bring To you and your kin; We wish you a mer-ry Christ-mas And a hap-py New Year.

Now bring us some figgy pudding,
Now bring us some figgy pudding,
Now bring us some figgy pudding,
And bring some out here. (*Chorus*)

For we all like figgy pudding,
We all like figgy pudding,
We all like figgy pudding,
So bring some out here. (*Chorus*)

And we won't go till we've got some,
We won't go till we've got some,
We won't go till we've got some,
So bring some out here. (*Chorus*)

19 Christingle

The Christingle is a traditional gift for children at Christmas. Many churches have special Christingle services, at which Christingles are given to children and everyone sings carols as the candles burn.

The different parts of the Christingle help tell the Christian story.

The orange stands for the world God made.

The sweets and fruits stand for all the good things the world provides, north, south, east and west.

The red ribbon stands for forgiveness. It is red like the colour of blood. When the baby Jesus grew up, he told people they must love and forgive one another. He said that they must do so because God loves and forgives people. Jealous enemies had Jesus put to death, nailed to a cross of wood. Still, as he hung bleeding, he forgave them. Christians believe that, in the same way, God forgives everyone.

The candle stands for Jesus. Christians believe that Jesus was God's Son, and he showed the world God's love. This love, they say, is light for the world.

You will need

an orange

double-sided tape

red ribbon

scissors

4 cocktail sticks

sweets and fruits

apple corer

kitchen foil (or Christmas foil)

candle

1 Wrap the double-sided tape around the middle of the orange.

2 Unpeel the backing and stick the ribbon in place on top of it. Tie a small knot to hold the ribbon tight and trim the ends.

3 Use the corer to make a candle-sized hole in the top of the orange.

4 Skewer sweets and fruits on the cocktail sticks and stick them into the orange.

5 Wrap foil around the bottom of the candle and push it firmly into the orange.

20 Christmas Love

The story of the very first Christmas is the story of Jesus being born. For Christians, the message is the one that Jesus gave: that God loves people, and that people are happy when they love God and one another.

Bright paper chains link many different colours. They can be a reminder at Christmas of how many different kinds of people can be joined together in love.

1 With ruler and pencil, mark strips 2 cm x 15 cm on your paper.

2 Lay the ruler along the line and pull upwards on the paper to tear it into strips 15 cm wide. Then lay the ruler on the other lines to tear off strips 2 cm wide. Make strips in different colours.

3 Take one strip and tape it into a circle.

4 Thread another strip through it and tape that into a circle. Add more strips to make your chain as long as you like.

Paper chains

You will need

coloured paper

ruler and pencil

sticky tape

A Christmas prayer

God, our loving Father, help us remember the birth of Jesus, that we may share in the song of the angels, the gladness of the shepherds, and the wisdom of the wise men.

Close the door of hate and open the door of love all over the world.

Let kindness come with every gift and good desires with every greeting.

Deliver us from evil by the blessing which Christ brings and teach us to be merry with clean hearts.

May the Christmas morning make us happy to be your children and the Christmas evening bring us to our beds with grateful thoughts, forgiving and forgiven, for Jesus' sake. Amen.

Robert Louis Stevenson (1850–94)

templates for Nativity characters on page 9

template for manger on page 9

template for envelope on page 4

template for woven heart on page 14

templates for decorations on page 4

Other titles from Lion Children's Books

First Festivals: Easter   *Lois Rock*

Lion Christmas Favourites   *compiled by Lois Rock*

The Christmas Story   *Lois Rock and Diana Mayo*